More Country Things

Other books by Bob Artley

Memories of a Former Kid

Cartoons

Cartoons II

A Country School

A Book of Chores

Ginny: A Love Remembered

Country Things

Country Christmas

MORE Country Things

BOB ARTLEY

IOWA STATE UNIVERSITY PRESS / AMES

Dedicated to those faithful readers who have expressed their appreciation of my work and thus have encouraged me to continue.

BOB ARTLEY, who studied art at Grinnell College and the University of Iowa, began his career as an editorial cartoonist with the *Des Moines Tribune.* He continued to draw for the two weekly papers he published with his wife, Ginny, and for the *Worthington* (Minnesota) *Daily Globe.* Now retired, Artley lives on the century farm in Hampton, Iowa, where he was born. There he finds inspiration for his writing and painting and draws weekly cartoons for syndication by Extra Newspaper Features.

© 1995 Bob Artley
All rights reserved

ACKNOWLEDGMENT. This book, like the first volume, is a selection from the syndicated series, "Country Things," distributed by Extra Newspaper Features, of Rochester, Minnesota, and appearing in publications in the United States and Canada.

No part of this book may be reproduced in any form or by any electronic or mechanical means, including information storage and retrieval systems, without written permission from the publisher, except for brief passages quoted in a review.

♾ Printed on acid-free paper in the United States of America

First edition, 1995

Library of Congress Cataloging-in-Publication Data

Artley, Bob.
    More country things / Bob Artley. — 1st ed.
        p.   cm.
    "This book, like the first volume [Country things] is a selection from the syndicated series, 'Country things'"—CIP galley.
    ISBN 0-8138-2451-6
    1. Country life—Pictorial works.   2. Farm equipment—Pictorial works.   3. Agricultural implements—Pictorial works.   4. Farm buildings—Pictorial works.   I. Title.
S521.A75   1995
977.7′009′7340222—dc20   95-22049

Contents

FOREWORD *by Herb Plambeck, vi*

PREFACE, *viii*

Spring, *2*

Summer, *36*

Autumn, *90*

Winter, *118*

Foreword

As a contemporary of Bob Artley, and a longtime admirer of his writings and his artistry, I deem it a privilege to be asked to write a foreword for *More Country Things*. In this his latest book, Bob is giving his readers, both old and new, a delightful and fascinating addition to his earlier books, such as *Memories of a Former Kid*, *Country Things*, and *Country Christmas*.

My own childhood experiences back in an earlier decade of this twentieth century are vividly recalled in this new book. As indicated in the Preface Artley has written, *More Country Things* is a collection of thoughts and drawings he has long wanted to express. In doing so, he is giving all of us an added Artley treasure.

In delineating the seasons of the year, Bob has captured highlights to which every reader can relate. Let me touch on a few items the author recalls for Spring, Summer, Autumn, and Winter. When the "former kid," as Artley often refers to himself, speaks of the first orange-tinted willow twigs in the spring, he also mentions the greening of pastures and lawns and the exhilarating cry of Canada geese winging their way northward in V formations. It seemed to me as though it had occurred only yesterday.

In Summer, he speaks of burgeoning crops in fields and gardens, the beauty of wildflowers, and sultry weather with its thunderstorms. And those of us who go back to Artley's boyhood days revel in his mention of threshing time and those bounteous, delicious meals farmwives prepared for the men and boys in the threshing crew. There's much else recalled. I especially enjoyed the "back to school time" that ended carefree summer days, as well as the harvest goal of finishing the corn-husking by Thanksgiving.

Of course, the Winter memories place the joyous Christmas holidays uppermost, but the snow and cold quickly come to mind. It was a time of bundling up, frostbite, and bad-tasting cold medicine, but also of sledding, skating, and skiing.

Artley also details hundreds of other seasonal memories enabling old-timers like me to reflect on happy childhood times; but he paints fascinating word pictures for younger generations as well.

In addition to the seasonal reminders, *More Country Things* has many pages of drawings as only Bob can draw them. They are a delightful depiction of many interesting observations. For example, maple sugar-making time shows the sap dripping through a tiny trough into the sugar bucket hung on the tree.

On another page, a mother hen is seen peering out of a little coop anxiously watching her chicks, ready to cluck them back into the building if any danger surfaces. The tiny coops of those long-ago days are a far cry from the huge buildings housing some 40,000 hens and equipped with automatic conveyor belts that take the eggs directly to the packaging room.

School days in older times are recalled in the picture of a little first-grader sitting on the country school's recitation bench, where he is struggling with a word in his book as he recites to the teacher, who has seven other grades to instruct.

Artley was a lad in pre-tractor years, when horses were still providing the power on the farm. One page shows the farmer with three horses on a sulky plow, an amazingly realistic portrayal of farm activity in the '20s and '30s. Still another picture shows the local blacksmith hard at work near his forge and anvil. Another scene shows a farmer with his team and wagon, loaded with cream cans, entering the local creamery.

I, too, write books, some of them also dealing with events and memories of the past. Thus, I know something about the time, thought, work, expense, and discipline Bob Artley has expended in the nine books he has written—and I salute him.

Last year my loving wife, Laura, gave me a first edition copy of Bob's *Country Christmas* as a much-appreciated Christmas gift. I can assure anyone and everyone that *Country Christmas*, like all of Bob's writings and drawings, offers pure enjoyment and I know this new book, *More Country Things*, will be equally well received.

If ever the Pulitzer Prize committee decides to award a Pulitzer to the nation's best evoker of times past in rural America, Bob Artley will be unanimously nominated for it. He richly deserves journalism's highest accolade.

Herb Plambeck

Veteran farm editor and broadcaster

Preface

When the first collection of cartoons, *Country Things*, was published in book form, I faced the difficult task of determining which drawings to include. I had done a great many more than I could use, and limitations of space simply wouldn't allow me to select all the worthy candidates. The selection process, always frustrating, was especially painful because many of those pieces I had to omit were of equal merit to the ones that "made it."

So I was especially gratified when a favorable response to the first book led to publishing another. That meant the drawings that were crowded out of the first book would have another chance. Yet there are still so many that I have been faced with the same problem of choosing one over another. How can anyone choose one of his children over another?

Why collect these cartoons into book form in the first place? The ready answer is that some readers who have followed the syndicated series "Country Things" suggested it. And since I was ripe for any excuse to do just that ... the first book became a reality. Now I hope those readers will enjoy *More Country Things* and its publication will also be vindicated.

One might also ask, why the interest in a book dealing with things that were once part of country life? My guess is that it has something to do with our longing for a time when life was simpler, when the values we lived by were well defined and supported by the community at large. It was a time when perhaps we knew better where we stood, where we came from, and who we were.

These country things are symbols or artifacts of that time—they are our connections to that life.

Artley Farm
Hampton, Iowa

More Country Things

Spring

From about Christmas on, we started watching the sun as it rose in the morning and set each night. Its slow march north along the horizon lengthened the days. January and February were considered the shank of the cold season, but March, with some balmy days followed by a sudden relapse into winter, could not be depended upon. Eventually, however, the snow and ice gave way to dripping eaves, slushy roads, muddy yards, and swollen streams.

First indications of the approach of the season of new life were the orange-tinged twigs of the willows. Lawns and pastures began greening, and the air was sweet with the smell of the pregnant earth.

When spring peepers sounded from the marshy areas of the lowlands, we took special notice and counted the number of times it frosted after we heard them. One of our experienced neighbors maintained, "Frogs have to freeze up three times before it's really spring."

The exhilarating wild cry of Canada geese came from high in the night sky as large flights of those majestic birds winged their way northward in V formations. We noted the sighting of the first robin, its rollicking warble proclaiming territorial rights. Flocks of blackbirds presented their disorganized, cacophonous concerts from the budding treetops.

As the season progressed, we watched for the arrival of killdeers, meadowlarks, swallows, and the busy little house wrens with their chittering chatter.

New birth was around us—calves, kittens, foals, lambs, piglets, and domestic fowl. These events on the farm had to be fitted in with spring fieldwork and gardening, tilling and planting, fence fixing and turning the cows into the verdant pasture as the tempo of the season picked up.

It was a wonderful time to be living close to the land.

MAPLE SYRUP-MAKING TIME, IN EARLY SPRING, IS WHEN ONE MIGHT SEE **SAP BUCKETS** HANGING ON TREES IN A MAPLE GROVE.

SPRING IS THE SEASON WHEN MANY EARTHY SCENTS ARE UP ON THE AIR. THE FAINT SMELL OF **SKUNK** IS ONE OF THEM — THE FAINTER THE BETTER — AN INDICATION THE LITTLE NIGHTTIME CREATURE IS AT A GREATER DISTANCE.

4

ONE OF THE GREAT JOYS OF COUNTRY LIVING IS SEEING AND HEARING THE MAJESTIC **CANADA GOOSE** IN ITS GREAT MIGRATORY FLIGHTS EACH SPRING AND FALL. ITS WILD CALL IS A TONIC TO A WEARY SPIRIT.

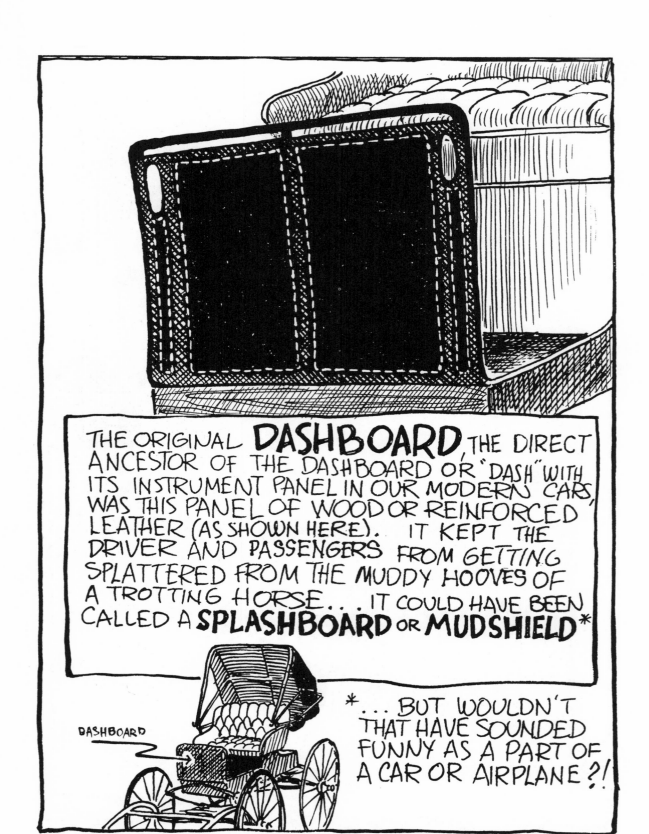

THE ORIGINAL **DASHBOARD**, THE DIRECT ANCESTOR OF THE DASHBOARD OR "DASH" WITH ITS INSTRUMENT PANEL IN OUR MODERN CARS, WAS THIS PANEL OF WOOD OR REINFORCED LEATHER (AS SHOWN HERE). IT KEPT THE DRIVER AND PASSENGERS FROM GETTING SPLATTERED FROM THE MUDDY HOOVES OF A TROTTING HORSE... IT COULD HAVE BEEN CALLED A **SPLASHBOARD** OR **MUDSHIELD** *

DASHBOARD

* ...BUT WOULDN'T THAT HAVE SOUNDED FUNNY AS A PART OF A CAR OR AIRPLANE?!

6

MAPLE SEEDS WERE ONE OF THE MANY RECURRING THINGS OF SPRING WE LOOKED FORWARD TO — THEY WERE INTENDED AS AN EFFECTIVE MEANS OF LETTING THE WIND HELP PROPAGATE THE MAPLE

...BUT WE FOUND THEM FUN FOR PLAY — (ESPECIALLY WHEN IN THE "JUICY" STAGE) TO "SNAP" IN AN UNSUSPECTING EAR.

SNAP!

ONE OF THE PERENNIAL JOYS OF SPRING FOR SMALL CHILDREN, AND THOSE FORTUNATE ADULTS WITH THE HEART OF A CHILD, IS THE LOWLY, UBIQUITOUS **DANDELION** WHOSE BRIGHT YELLOW PRESENCE BRIGHTENS GRASSY HILLSIDES AND LAWNS AND DRIVES THE FASTIDIOUS GARDENER FOR THE DIGGING FORK ... OR HERBICIDE.

ABOUT THIS TIME OF YEAR IN ITS COOL, DARK CORNER OF THE CELLAR, THE **POTATO**, IN RESPONSE TO URGENT LIFE FORCES, PUTS FORTH TENDER, PALE SPROUTS AND SEEMS TO BE SAYING, "HURRY, GET ME PLANTED!"

SEED POTATOES CUT INTO PIECES WITH AT LEAST 2 EYES →

The DISTINCTIVE, PIERCING CRY OF THE UBIQUITOUS **KILLDEER**, PROBABLY THE BEST KNOWN SHOREBIRD IN NORTH AMERICA, CAN BE HEARD IN FLIGHT OR ON THE GROUND, IN MEADOWS, CULTIVATED FIELDS OR OPEN GRAVELLY PLACES, WHERE IT BUILDS ITS SIMPLE NEST — A SLIGHT DEPRESSION SURROUNDED WITH A FEW PEBBLES.

ONE OF THE PERENNIAL CHORES ON THE FARM WAS **REPAIRING** THE **CREEK FENCES** AFTER THE RAVAGES OF WINTER STORMS AND SPRING FLOODS.

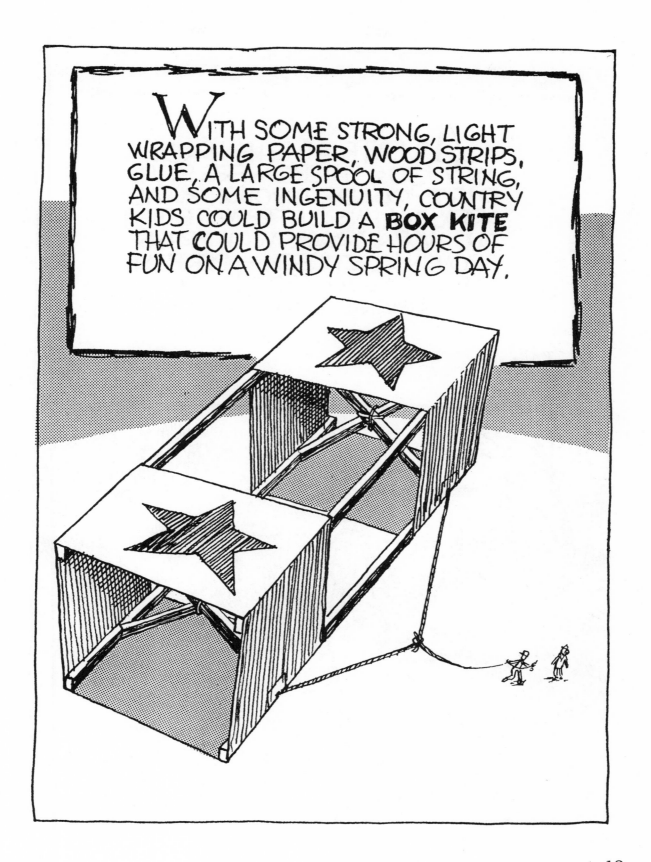

WITH SOME STRONG, LIGHT WRAPPING PAPER, WOOD STRIPS, GLUE, A LARGE SPOOL OF STRING, AND SOME INGENUITY, COUNTRY KIDS COULD BUILD A **BOX KITE** THAT COULD PROVIDE HOURS OF FUN ON A WINDY SPRING DAY.

As LATE AS THE 1920s AND '30s, THERE WERE STILL **DIRT ROADS** THROUGH RURAL AREAS THAT WERE LITTLE MORE THAN TWO WORN TRACKS WITH GRASS GROWING BETWEEN — PERFECT FOR A LEISURELY STROLL ON A FINE SPRING DAY.

It seemed that **RENDERING LARD** from pig fat, after the end-of-winter hog butchering, was one of the rites of spring on the farm. This was usually done outdoors.

16

THE FOUR-QUART **GLASS CHURN** WAS USED IN MAKING BUTTER FOR HOME USE.

THE PADDLE WAS MADE OF HARD MAPLE WOOD.

IT COULD ALSO BE USED AS A MIXER FOR BAKING CAKES, ETC.

THERE WERE FEW DELIGHTS THAT COULD MATCH THAT OF COMING INTO A FARM KITCHEN WHEN HOMEMADE **BAKING POWDER BISCUITS** HAD JUST BEEN TAKEN OUT OF THE RANGE OVEN — AND THEN TO SAMPLE THE SCRUMPTIOUS MORSELS WITH BUTTER AND HONEY OR JAM.

At the edge of groves or in the corners of fence rows there were **ROCK PILES** that "GREW" year after year — but not without back-breaking effort as the rocks were gleaned from the cultivated fields.

Often present in a back corner of a well-kept garden is the **COMPOST HEAP**, where grass clippings, leaves, garden waste and kitchen scraps (not meat) are dumped. There are many composting methods, all of which biologically convert this waste material into nutrient-filled soil for the garden.

BEFORE THE WIDESPREAD USE OF CHEMICALS IN FARMING, THE UBIQUITOUS **MANURE PILE** WAS AN IMPORTANT RESOURCE THAT, TOGETHER WITH THE PRACTICE OF THE ROTATION OF CROPS, HELPED TO KEEP THE SOIL HEALTHY AND PRODUCTIVE YEAR AFTER YEAR.

22

BEFORE THE PREVALENCE OF **V** BELTS IN FARM MACHINERY, SPROCKET CHAINS WERE USED TO TRANSFER POWER FROM ONE SHAFT TO ANOTHER.

THE STEEL **CHAIN DETACHER**, SHOWN HERE, WAS A TOOL USED TO DETACH AND ADD LINKS TO THE SPROCKET CHAINS.

SPROCKET CHAIN LINKS

STEEL CHAIN DETACHER

Most individual chicken coops for a mother hen and her chicks were probably homemade of wood. However, there were manufactured **SHEET METAL COOPS** on the market that had many advantages — one of them being that they were more rodent-proof.

25

ONE OF THE MANY ATTRAC-
TIONS OF SPRING WAS LOOKING
FOR (AND FINDING) A NEST OF
NEW KITTENS — SOMETIMES
UP IN THE HAYMOW BACK UNDER
THE EAVES.

When family farms predominated in the rural landscape, and most of them had a small dairy herd, many a small town had a **CREAMERY** to which the farmers brought their cream to be made into butter — the byproduct, buttermilk, was sometimes hauled back to the farms to be fed to the pigs.

This creamery at Latimer, Iowa, in the early part of this century was later replaced by a brick building.

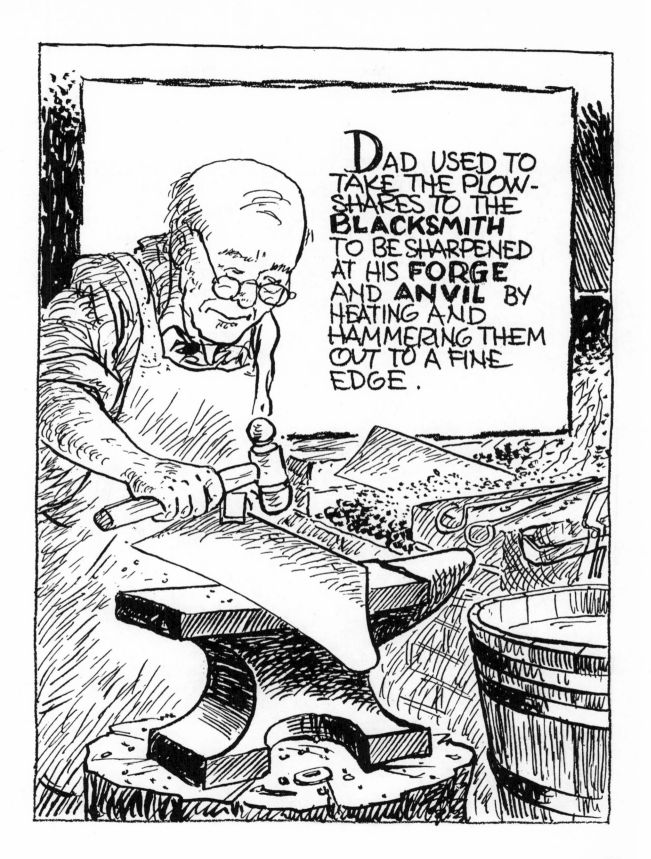

DAD USED TO TAKE THE PLOW-SHARES TO THE **BLACKSMITH** TO BE SHARPENED AT HIS **FORGE** AND **ANVIL** BY HEATING AND HAMMERING THEM OUT TO A FINE EDGE.

Spring in the fields used to consist mostly of the **QUIET SOUNDS** of birds, the wind in the grasses, and the muffled step of the horses in their creaking harnesses, and the grating of pebbles against the steel moldboard of the plow as it sliced through the black prairie loam.

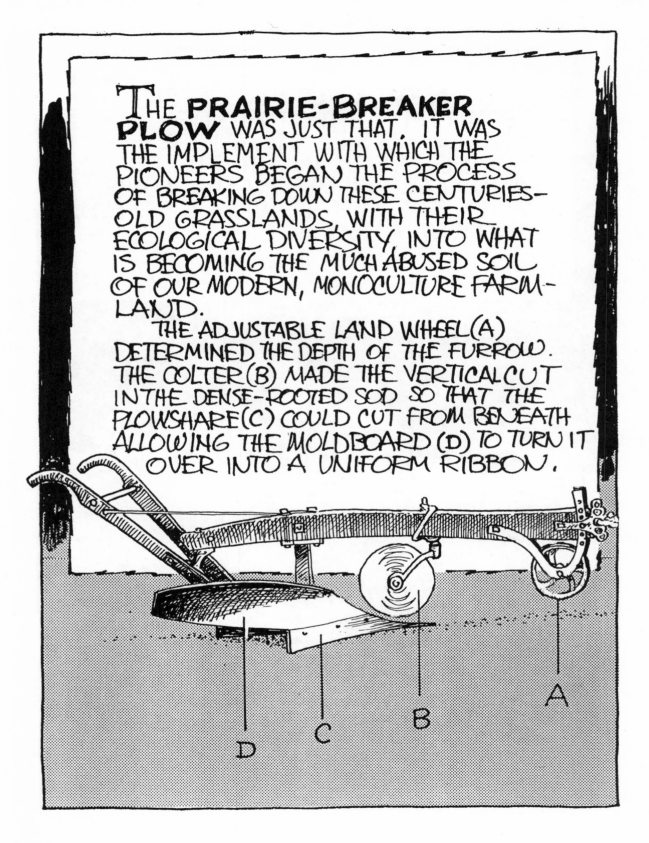

The **PRAIRIE-BREAKER PLOW** WAS JUST THAT. IT WAS THE IMPLEMENT WITH WHICH THE PIONEERS BEGAN THE PROCESS OF BREAKING DOWN THESE CENTURIES-OLD GRASSLANDS, WITH THEIR ECOLOGICAL DIVERSITY, INTO WHAT IS BECOMING THE MUCH ABUSED SOIL OF OUR MODERN, MONOCULTURE FARM-LAND.

THE ADJUSTABLE LAND WHEEL(A) DETERMINED THE DEPTH OF THE FURROW. THE COLTER (B) MADE THE VERTICAL CUT IN THE DENSE-ROOTED SOD SO THAT THE PLOWSHARE (C) COULD CUT FROM BENEATH ALLOWING THE MOLDBOARD (D) TO TURN IT OVER INTO A UNIFORM RIBBON.

D C B A

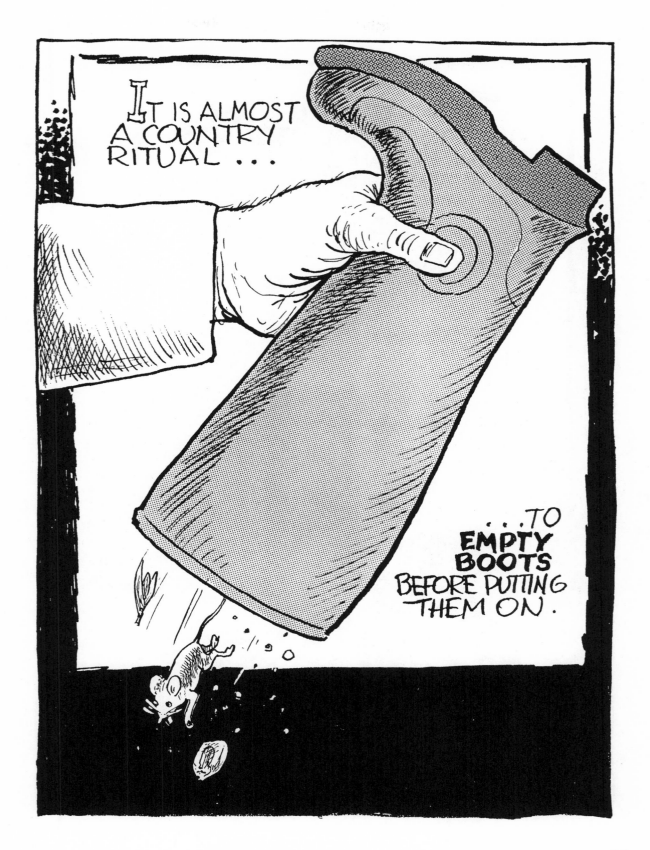

THE HORSE-PULLED DISC HAD **HARDWOOD BEARINGS.** IN THE TOP HALF OF EACH SET OF BEARINGS WAS A HOLE THROUGH WHICH CUP GREASE WAS FORCED TO LUBRICATE THE SHAFT THAT PASSED THROUGH IT.

BEFORE THERE WERE GREASE GUNS AND GREASE FITTINGS, OR FACTORY-SEALED BEARINGS WITH BUILT-IN LUBRICATION, THERE WAS, ON FARM MACHINERY, A **GREASE CUP** AT EACH BEARING. THESE CUPS NEEDED TO BE FILLED REGULARLY.

WOODEN PADDLE

GREASE CUP SCREWS DOWN TO FORCE GREASE...

...DOWN THROUGH TUBE TO BEARING ON SHAFT

CUP GREASE

Summer

The flow of spring into summer, a little past the middle of June, was subtle. Gradually, the warmth of the sun, now at its highest in the sky, was becoming overbearing. Thunderstorms, followed by steamy, sultry days were the usual fare. Field crops and gardens burgeoned, and so did the wildflowers ... and weeds.

The air of the countryside was likely to be heavy with the heady scent of freshly cut hay, and barn mows were bulging with the fragrant new crop. Single or two-row cultivators, pulled by large, plodding draft horses, moved slowly across the field of dark green rows of corn. The lone operator perched on the iron seat with the reins looped over one shoulder, across the back, and around under the other arm. The hands grasped the wooden handles, guiding the shovels that turned the warm, loamy soil up around the base of the corn plants, covering the emerging grass and weeds that were trying to take over the field.

It was the time of oat harvesting—first cutting and shocking and then the exciting time of threshing, when neighbors came together to exchange work until each farm's crop was gathered and stored for the year's feed supply.

Summer, when we were young, was going to town on Saturday night to trade eggs, butter, or cream for groceries that were not produced on the farm. It was Fourth of July celebrations, family picnics, vacations, sandlot baseball games, swimming, and lolling in a hammock.

Summer was also a time for building or making repairs around the farmstead—a time for taking up the slack.

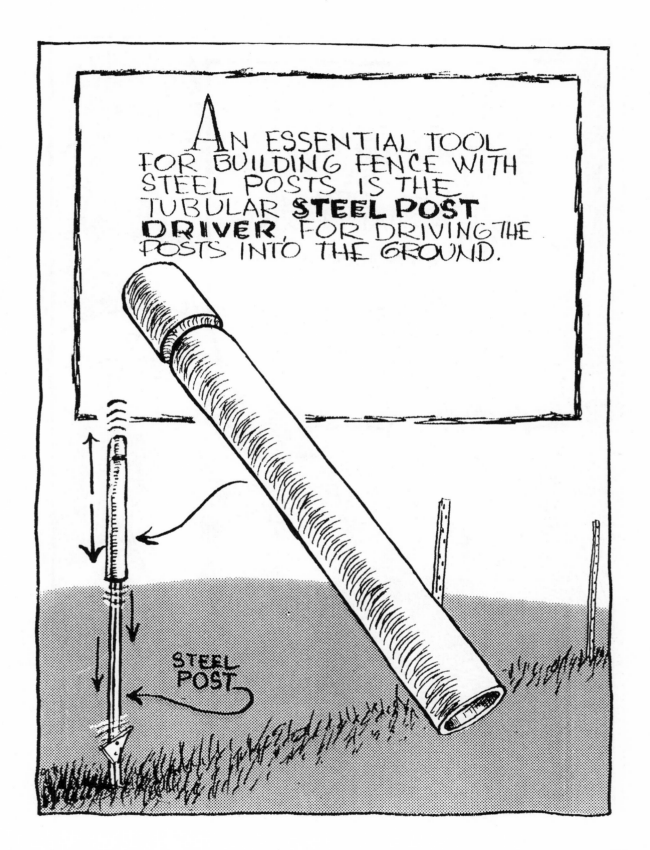

An essential tool for building fence with steel posts is the tubular **STEEL POST DRIVER**, for driving the posts into the ground.

STEEL POST

40

A ROAD CULVERT MADE AN INTERESTING PLACE TO EXPLORE IN SOME OF OUR SUMMER EXCURSIONS AROUND THE FARM AND COUNTRYSIDE WHEN WE WERE KIDS.

When poking about in barns or sheds this time of year, one is apt to come upon a huge, gray, hairy **BARN SPIDER** that is waiting patiently for a fly to become entangled in its web.

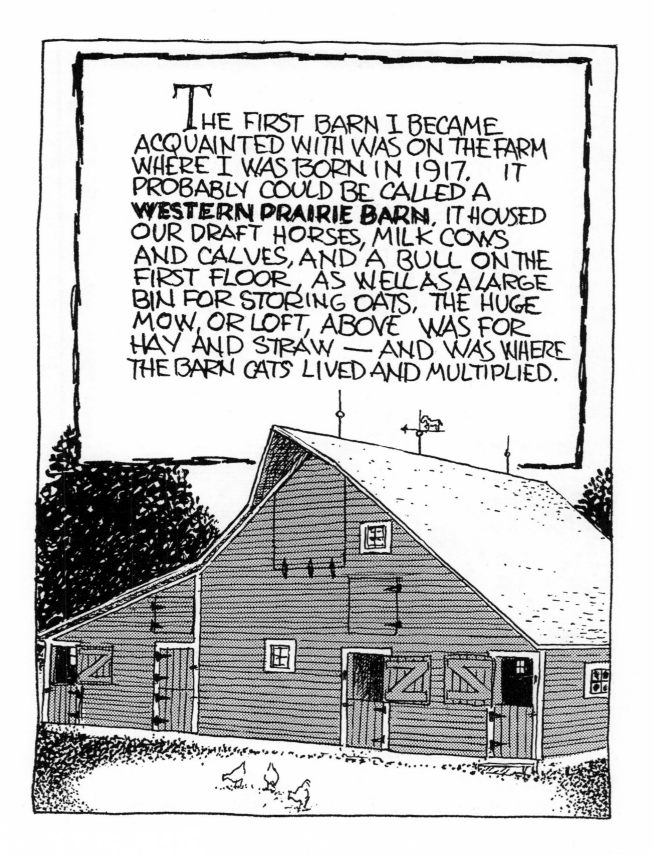

THE FIRST BARN I BECAME ACQUAINTED WITH WAS ON THE FARM WHERE I WAS BORN IN 1917. IT PROBABLY COULD BE CALLED A **WESTERN PRAIRIE BARN**. IT HOUSED OUR DRAFT HORSES, MILK COWS AND CALVES, AND A BULL ON THE FIRST FLOOR, AS WELL AS A LARGE BIN FOR STORING OATS. THE HUGE MOW, OR LOFT, ABOVE WAS FOR HAY AND STRAW — AND WAS WHERE THE BARN CATS LIVED AND MULTIPLIED.

On top of most barns, and other buildings that housed livestock, were wooden cupolas or, as shown here, **METAL VENTILATORS**.

Back when family farms were much more self-sufficient, most of the work was done by hand using tools which in many cases, like this **WOODEN HAY RAKE**, were made by hand right on the farm where it was used.

PICTURED HERE IS A TOY **HAY STACKER** THAT IS A FAIR REPLICA OF THE REAL THING THAT WAS USED AT HAY-MAKING TIME UP INTO THE EARLY 1900s.

A PIECE OF EQUIPMENT FOR HANDLING EITHER LOOSE OR BALED HAY IS THE **GRAPPLE FORK**. USED TOGETHER WITH PULLEYS AND ROPES, IT CAN LIFT LARGE BITES OF HAY FROM THE WAGON INTO THE HAY-LOFT OF THE BARN.

THE **GREAT DOOR** OF THE HAY-MOW WAS OPENED ONLY IN THE HAYING SEASON WHEN LOADS OF LOOSE CLOVER, TIMOTHY, OR ALFALFA HAY WERE HOISTED THROUGH IT INTO THE MOW FOR STORAGE FOR WINTER FEED.

Before the widespread use of herbicides, when weeds were controlled by the rotation of crops and tillage of the soil, an implement such as this horse-drawn **SINGLE ROW CULTIVATOR**, was an essential piece of equipment on every farm.

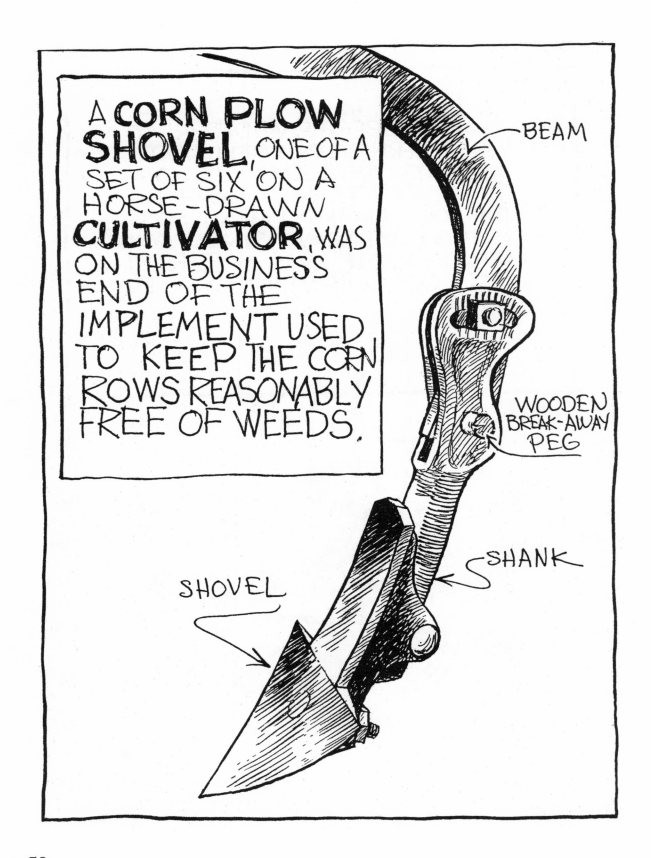

A **CORN PLOW SHOVEL**, ONE OF A SET OF SIX ON A HORSE-DRAWN **CULTIVATOR**, WAS ON THE BUSINESS END OF THE IMPLEMENT USED TO KEEP THE CORN ROWS REASONABLY FREE OF WEEDS.

BEAM

WOODEN BREAK-AWAY PEG

SHANK

SHOVEL

TODAY'S CONCEPTS OF COMFORT WERE NOT A CONSIDERATION WHEN HORSE-DRAWN FARM IMPLEMENTS WERE DESIGNED. THE ROUGHLY CONTOURED **METAL SEAT** WAS SIMPLY A PRACTICAL PLACE FOR THE DRIVER/OPERATOR TO PERCH.

SOMETIMES "CUSHIONED COMFORT" WAS IMPROVISED WITH A GUNNY SACK STUFFED WITH STRAW.

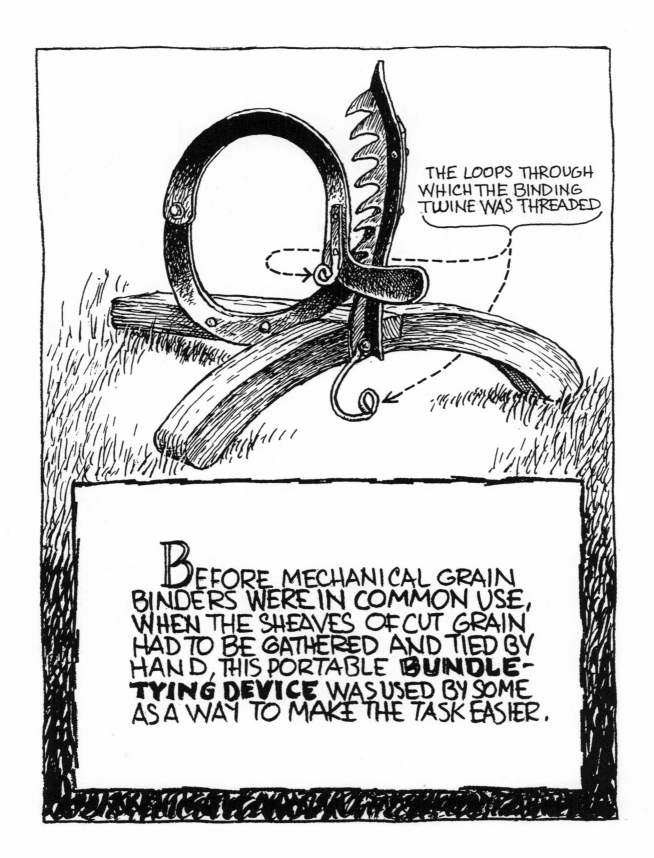

52

EVEN THOUGH IT WAS USED BUT A SHORT WHILE EACH YEAR, THE **BINDER APRON** WAS NEEDED TO MOVE THE STALKS OF CUT GRAIN (OATS, WHEAT, BARLEY, ETC.) THROUGH THE MACHINE THAT BOUND THEM INTO BUNDLES.

THOUGH IT WAS MADE OF A RUGGED COTTON CANVAS MATERIAL, IT REQUIRED AT LEAST ANNUAL MAINTENANCE AND REPAIR.

HARD WOOD CLEATS (RIVETED TO THE CANVAS)

STRAPS OF WEBBED BELTING

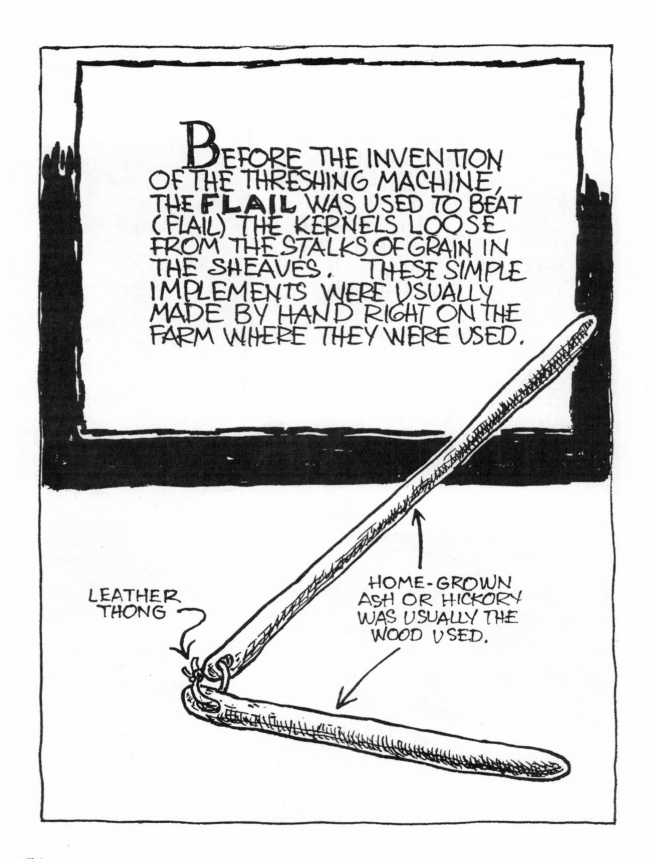

BEFORE THE INVENTION OF THE THRESHING MACHINE, THE **FLAIL** WAS USED TO BEAT (FLAIL) THE KERNELS LOOSE FROM THE STALKS OF GRAIN IN THE SHEAVES. THESE SIMPLE IMPLEMENTS WERE USUALLY MADE BY HAND RIGHT ON THE FARM WHERE THEY WERE USED.

LEATHER THONG

HOME-GROWN ASH OR HICKORY WAS USUALLY THE WOOD USED.

STILL OCCASIONALLY TO BE FOUND IN MUSEUMS OR IN THE DUSTY CORNERS OF OLD GRANARIES OR BARNS OF ANCIENT FARMS, IS THE **WINNOWING SIEVE**. THIS PRIMITIVE HAND-TOOL, WITH THE HELP OF WIND, WAS USED TO SEPARATE CHAFF AND DIRT FROM THRESHED GRAIN.
MODERN THRESHING MACHINES (COMBINES) STILL USE THIS PRINCIPLE.

CHAFF AND DIRT

WINNOWED GRAIN

THRESHED GRAIN

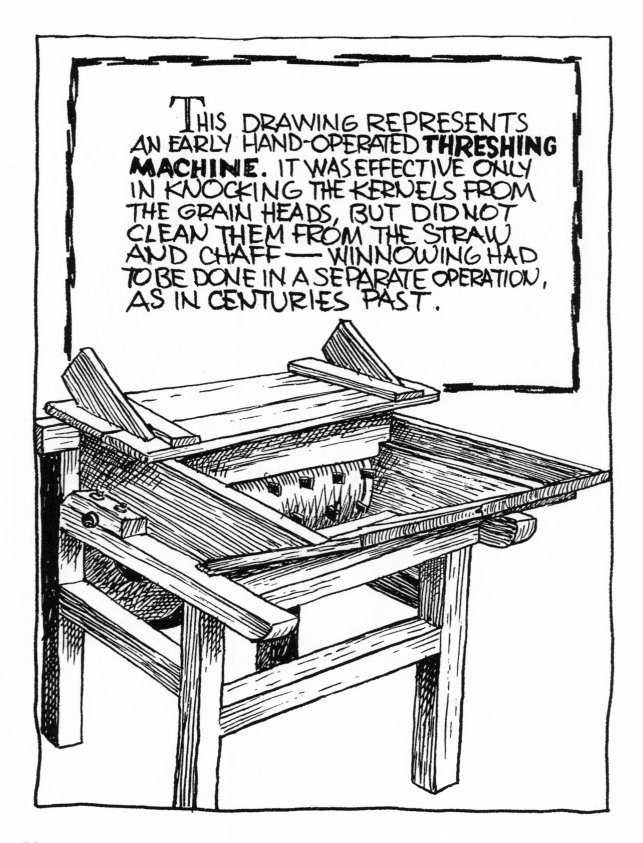

THIS DRAWING REPRESENTS AN EARLY HAND-OPERATED **THRESHING MACHINE**. IT WAS EFFECTIVE ONLY IN KNOCKING THE KERNELS FROM THE GRAIN HEADS, BUT DID NOT CLEAN THEM FROM THE STRAW AND CHAFF — WINNOWING HAD TO BE DONE IN A SEPARATE OPERATION, AS IN CENTURIES PAST.

IN THE DAYS WHEN THE THRESHING WAS DONE BY STEAM POWER, THE **WATER WAGON** WAS AN ESSENTIAL PART OF THE THRESHING RIG. FILLED BY MEANS OF A HAND PUMP, BY THE "WATER MONKEY," FROM THE FARM STOCK TANK, IT WAS PULLED BY HORSES TO WHERE IT COULD GIVE THE STEAM ENGINE A CONSTANT SUPPLY OF WATER TO BE CONVERTED INTO STEAM.

At threshing time, we had to gather up the **BIN BOARDS** scattered about the farm, and put them into place in the oats bin to contain the summer's new crop.

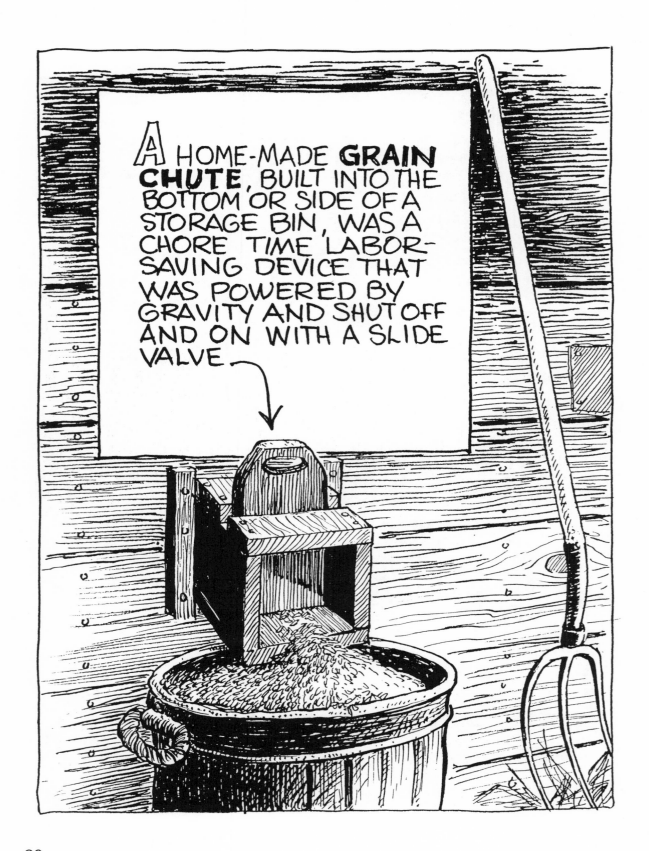

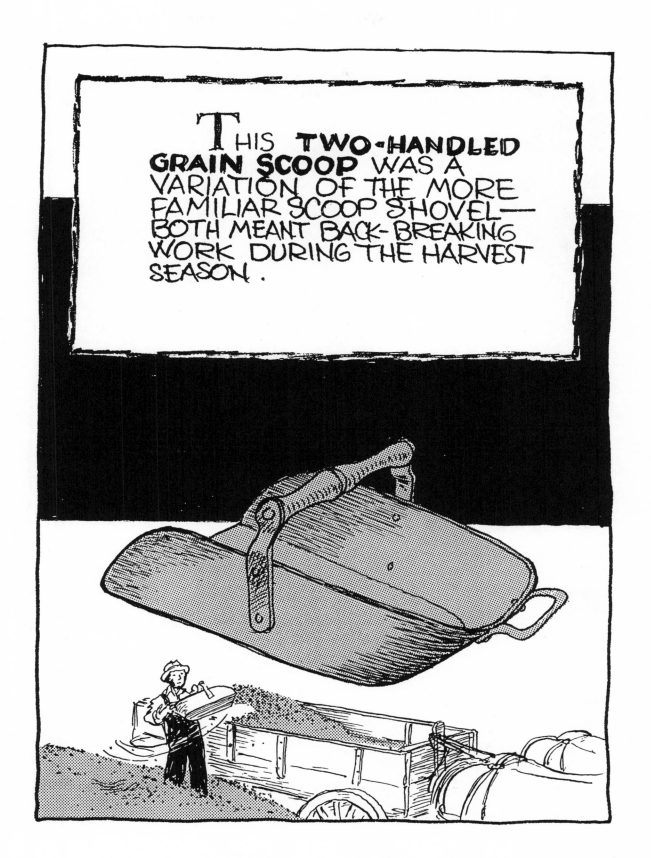

THIS **TWO-HANDLED GRAIN SCOOP** WAS A VARIATION OF THE MORE FAMILIAR SCOOP SHOVEL— BOTH MEANT BACK-BREAKING WORK DURING THE HARVEST SEASON.

RATS AND MICE WERE NOT THE ONLY CREATURES FOUND IN BIG, OLD BARNS — THERE ALSO MIGHT BE THE SECRETIVE **BARN OWL**, ARCHENEMY OF THE RESIDENT RODENTS, UPON WHICH IT LIKED TO FEED.

A TOOL NOT LIKELY TO BE FOUND IN A MODERN WOOD-WORKING SHOP, BUT VALUED BY COLLECTORS, IS THE **CARPENTER'S ADZE**. THIS TOOL, IN THE HANDS OF A SKILLED CRAFTSMAN, COULD HEW A SMOOTH-SURFACED BEAM.

ROUGH SURFACE MADE BY A BROADAXE

In the summertime, after milking (morning and night) the milk pails were washed and hung on the **DRYING RACK** to air dry.

A PLATFORM SCALE, SUCH AS THE ONE SHOWN HERE, WAS AN IMPORTANT PIECE OF EQUIPMENT AT CREAMERIES, MILK-BUYING STATIONS, AND ON SOME DAIRY FARMS.

One of the most intelligent domestic animals on the farm is the **PIG**. But at the same time it is probably the most obnoxious — with its gross life-style, its sometimes vicious nature and its constant inclination to escape.

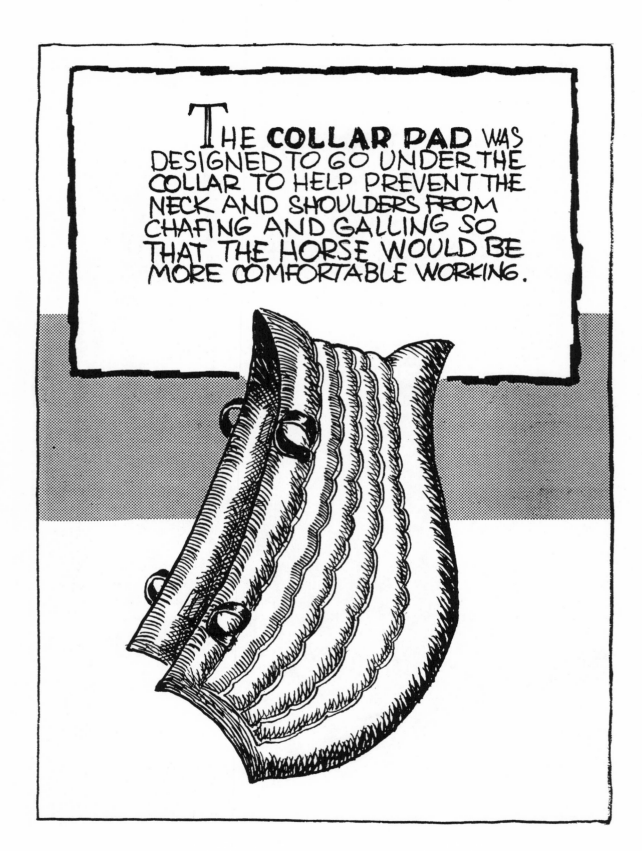

THE **COLLAR PAD** WAS DESIGNED TO GO UNDER THE COLLAR TO HELP PREVENT THE NECK AND SHOULDERS FROM CHAFING AND GALLING SO THAT THE HORSE WOULD BE MORE COMFORTABLE WORKING.

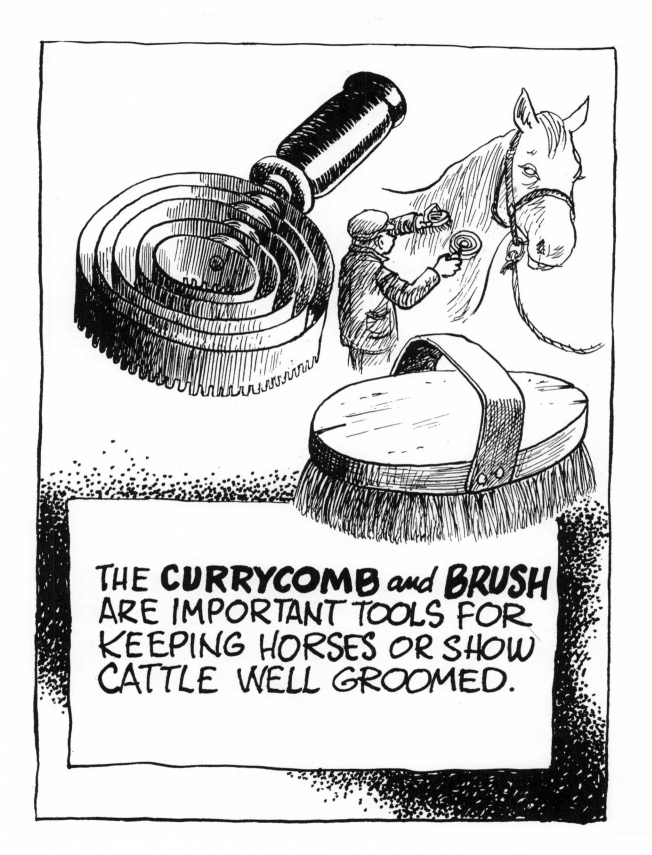

THE **CURRYCOMB** and **BRUSH** ARE IMPORTANT TOOLS FOR KEEPING HORSES OR SHOW CATTLE WELL GROOMED.

In the heat of the summer months, on farms without 'ice boxes or refrigerators, perishable foods like butter, milk, cream, cheese and eggs, often were kept in **EARTHENWARE CROCKS** on the cellar's dirt floor.

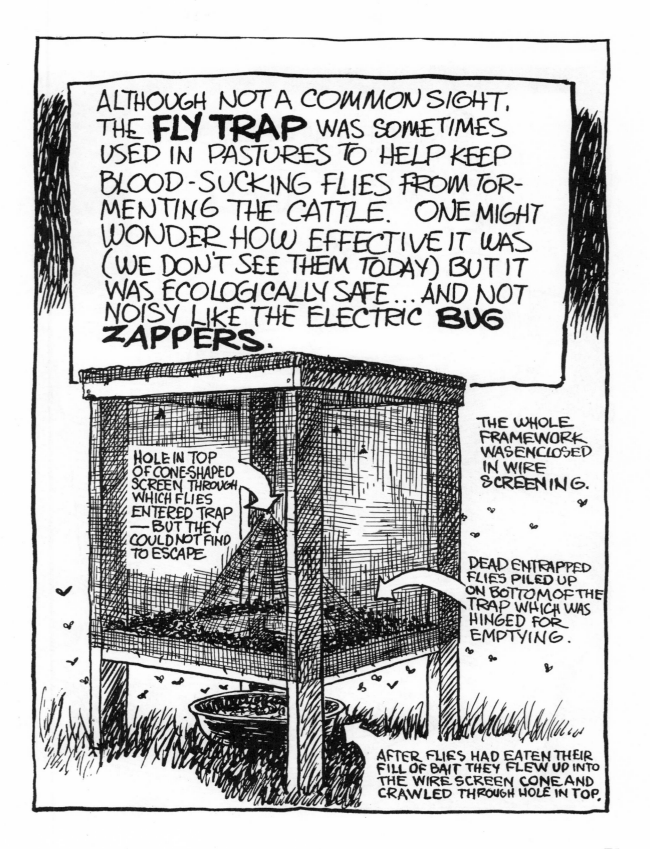

ALTHOUGH NOT A COMMON SIGHT, THE **FLY TRAP** WAS SOMETIMES USED IN PASTURES TO HELP KEEP BLOOD-SUCKING FLIES FROM TORMENTING THE CATTLE. ONE MIGHT WONDER HOW EFFECTIVE IT WAS (WE DON'T SEE THEM TODAY) BUT IT WAS ECOLOGICALLY SAFE... AND NOT NOISY LIKE THE ELECTRIC **BUG ZAPPERS.**

HOLE IN TOP OF CONE-SHAPED SCREEN THROUGH WHICH FLIES ENTERED TRAP — BUT THEY COULD NOT FIND TO ESCAPE

THE WHOLE FRAMEWORK WAS ENCLOSED IN WIRE SCREENING.

DEAD ENTRAPPED FLIES PILED UP ON BOTTOM OF THE TRAP WHICH WAS HINGED FOR EMPTYING.

AFTER FLIES HAD EATEN THEIR FILL OF BAIT THEY FLEW UP INTO THE WIRE SCREEN CONE AND CRAWLED THROUGH HOLE IN TOP.

71

ONE OF THE GREATEST DELIGHTS OF SUMMER WAS/IS THE FIRST FRESH, HOME-MADE **APPLE PIE.**

ON SOME FARMS, OFTEN IN AN OUT-OF-THE-WAY CORNER OF THE BARNYARD, WAS A SHALLOW **DUCK POND** FOR THE HEALTH AND HAPPINESS OF THE DOMESTIC WATERFOWL.

A WAY OF FEEDING A HORSE, WHEN IT WAS ON THE JOB, WAS TO PUT ON A **FEED BAG** MADE OF CANVAS AND LEATHER. A MEASURE OF GRAIN WAS PUT INTO THIS BAG AND THEN SLIPPED OVER THE HORSE'S MUZZLE.

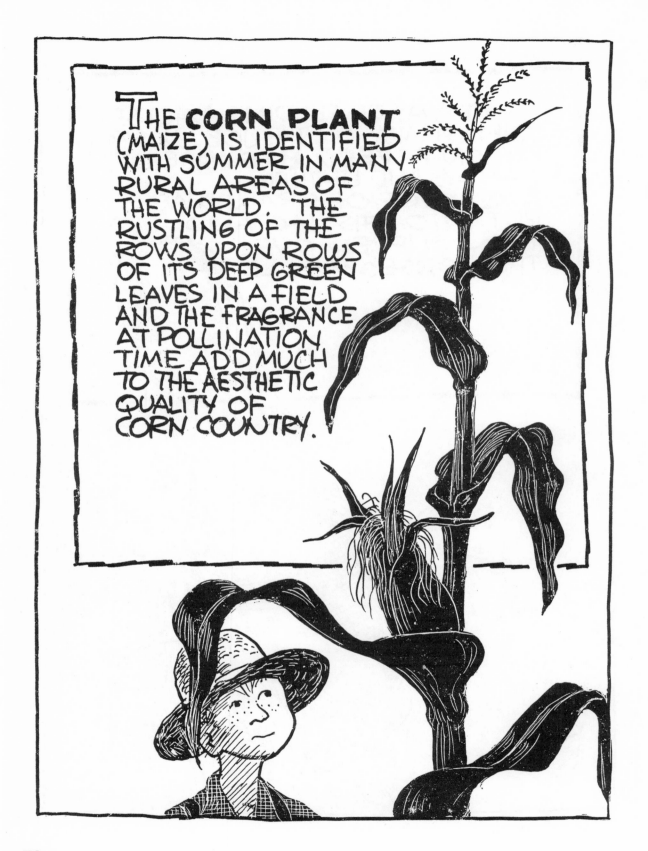

THE **CORN PLANT** (MAIZE) IS IDENTIFIED WITH SUMMER IN MANY RURAL AREAS OF THE WORLD. THE RUSTLING OF THE ROWS UPON ROWS OF ITS DEEP GREEN LEAVES IN A FIELD AND THE FRAGRANCE AT POLLINATION TIME ADD MUCH TO THE AESTHETIC QUALITY OF CORN COUNTRY.

A USED CAR TIRE, A LENGTH OF HEMP ROPE, AND A WELL-PLACED TREE LIMB COMBINED TO MAKE A **TIRE SWING** FOR HOURS OF SUMMER FUN.

Some of the most enjoyable playthings were those that were homemade. An old **WAGON WHEEL**, mounted on a partly buried axle, made a **MERRY-GO-ROUND** that provided hours of outdoor fun for the little ones.

TWO IRON STAKES, DRIVEN INTO THE GROUND FORTY FEET APART, AND TWO HORSESHOES FOR EACH PLAYER, IS ALL THE EQUIPMENT THAT IS NEEDED FOR A PLEASANT, SUMMERY AFTERNOON **GAME OF HORSESHOES**.

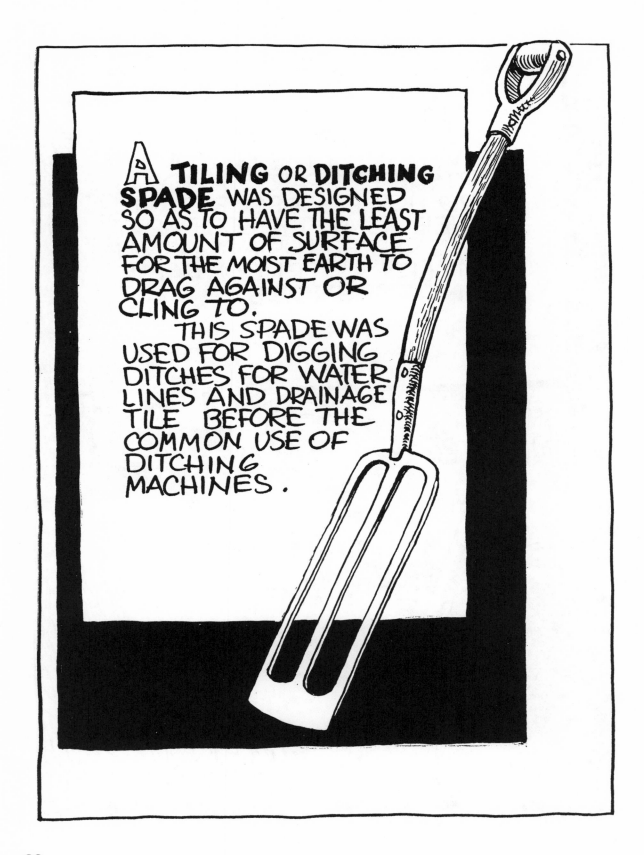

A TILING OR DITCHING SPADE WAS DESIGNED SO AS TO HAVE THE LEAST AMOUNT OF SURFACE FOR THE MOIST EARTH TO DRAG AGAINST OR CLING TO.

THIS SPADE WAS USED FOR DIGGING DITCHES FOR WATER LINES AND DRAINAGE TILE BEFORE THE COMMON USE OF DITCHING MACHINES.

THE **CRUMBER** WAS A TOOL USED IN THE LAYING OF DRAINAGE TILE TO SMOOTH AND CLEAN THE BOTTOM OF THE DITCH SO THAT THE TILES WOULD LIE LEVEL.

THE **TILING HOOK** WAS A LONG-HANDLED TOOL THAT WAS USED TO LOWER INDIVIDUAL SECTIONS OF THE CLAY DRAINAGE TILES INTO PLACE AT THE BOTTOM OF THE DITCH THAT HAD BEEN DUG FOR THEM.

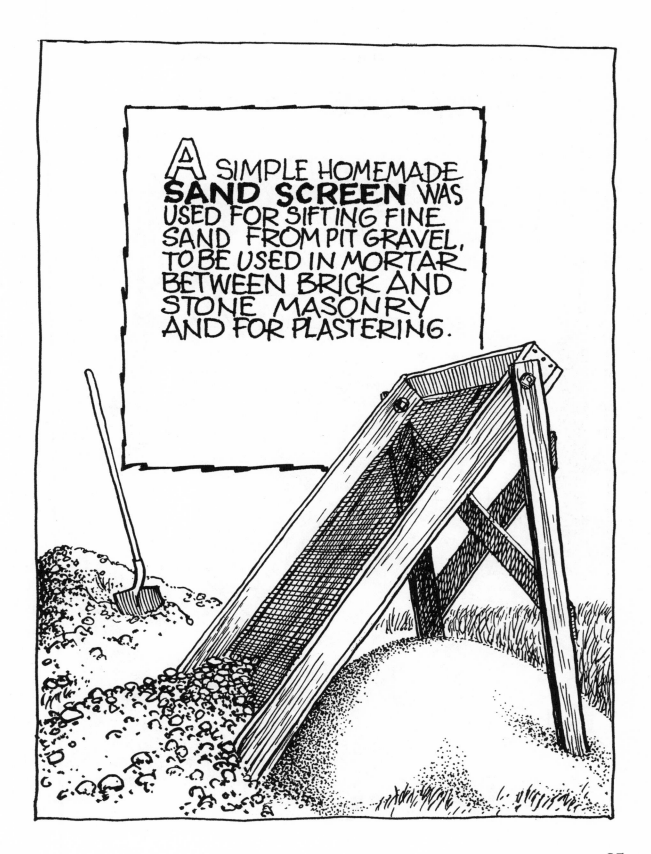

A SIMPLE HOMEMADE **SAND SCREEN** WAS USED FOR SIFTING FINE SAND FROM PIT GRAVEL, TO BE USED IN MORTAR BETWEEN BRICK AND STONE MASONRY AND FOR PLASTERING.

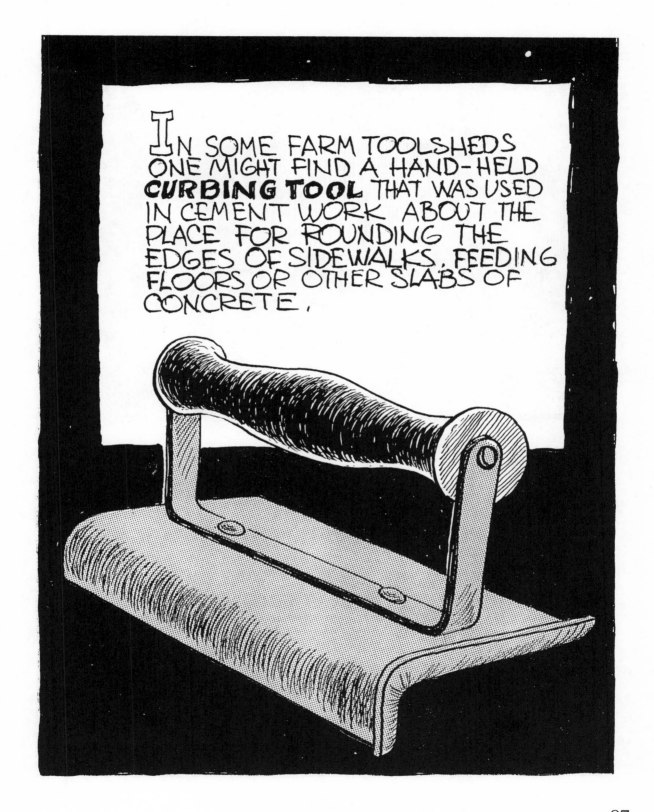

IN SOME FARM TOOLSHEDS ONE MIGHT FIND A HAND-HELD **CURBING TOOL** THAT WAS USED IN CEMENT WORK ABOUT THE PLACE FOR ROUNDING THE EDGES OF SIDEWALKS, FEEDING FLOORS OR OTHER SLABS OF CONCRETE.

Back when most rural roads crossed streams on wooden structures, instead of steel or concrete, a roof and sides were built over them as protection against the elements. Thus the picturesque **COVERED BRIDGE** came into being.

The one shown here is near the town of Winterset, Iowa.

Autumn

There was a definite demarcation between summer and autumn when we were small—it was when the new school year began.

The open, carefree days of summer vacation came to an end. Schedules were again imposed on our lives as routines were re-established for school and community organizations. Harvesting, which had begun in the summer with hay, small grains, and garden produce, was intensified with the urgency to prepare for winter.

Potatoes were dug and stored in the cellar. Corn silage was chopped and put into the silo. The ripened corn was cut, bound into bundles, and set into shocks in the field to dry, later to be hauled to the farmyard and piled into stacks or run through the shredding machine. This process separated the whole ears from the fodder, which was shredded and heaped in stacks or barns for winter livestock feed and bedding.

The final crop to be brought in from the fields was the ear corn that had been drying in its husks on ripened stalks. It was picked by hand (until the mechanical corn picker was developed), one ear at a time, and thrown into a wagon that was pulled back and forth across the same fields by the same draft horses that had pulled the cultivator just a few months before.

Thanksgiving time, the target date to finish corn picking, was a wonderful feast when we could truly give thanks to God for the bounty of the fields, gardens, and orchards.

And finally, after the crops were gathered and stored, firewood was cut and brought to the house for ready access. We were ready for and looked forward to the coming of winter and the advent of Christmas, that bright star of joy and hope in the darkest time of the year.

ABOUT IN SEPTEMBER THE YOUNG **PULLETS** WERE MATURE ENOUGH TO BE MOVED INTO THEIR **LAYING QUARTERS**, WHERE NESTS WERE PROVIDED FOR THEM TO USE WHEN READY TO START PRODUCING EGGS.

After being silent all summer long, the **COUNTRY SCHOOL BELL**, high in its tower, again sounded its urgent musical summons in the crisp autumn air.

When deemed necessary, school transportation in rural areas during the first part of this century was often by means of a homemade **SCHOOL BUS** mounted on a light truck or car chassis.

A FORMER SYRUP PAIL WAS OFTEN PRESSED INTO SERVICE AS A **LUNCH BUCKET** WHEN WE ATTENDED COUNTRY SCHOOL DURING THE 1920s AND 1930s.

95

IN EARLY AUTUMN THERE WERE USUALLY A FEW **SELECT CORN EARS** ON DISPLAY ABOUT THE FARMSTEAD AS TROPHIES FROM THE FIELDS ABOUT TO BE HARVESTED.

B EFORE MECHANICAL CORN PICKERS AND COMBINES CAME INTO USE, HOGS WERE SOMETIMES EMPLOYED TO HARVEST THEIR OWN FEED BY TURNING THEM INTO A FENCED-OFF FIELD TO "**HOG DOWN**" STANDING, RIPE CORN.

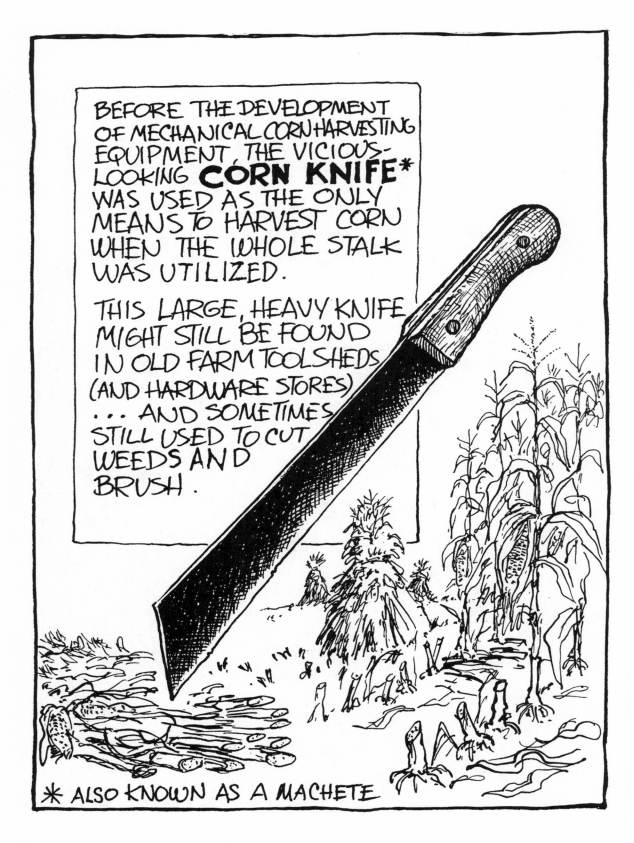

BEFORE THE DEVELOPMENT OF MECHANICAL CORN HARVESTING EQUIPMENT, THE VICIOUS-LOOKING **CORN KNIFE*** WAS USED AS THE ONLY MEANS TO HARVEST CORN WHEN THE WHOLE STALK WAS UTILIZED.

THIS LARGE, HEAVY KNIFE MIGHT STILL BE FOUND IN OLD FARM TOOLSHEDS (AND HARDWARE STORES) ... AND SOMETIMES STILL USED TO CUT WEEDS AND BRUSH.

* ALSO KNOWN AS A MACHETE

CORN HUSKS, EMPTY OF THEIR EARS, ARE APT TO BE SEEN ALMOST ANYWHERE IN CORN COUNTRY IN AUTUMN — IN FIELDS AND FARM-YARDS OR BLOWING ACROSS ROADS. BUT EVEN THESE EMPTY HUSKS ARE NOT WITHOUT VALUE; THEY MAKE GOOD CATTLE FODDER AND IN EARLY DAYS THEY WERE USED IN MANY WAYS SUCH AS STUFFING FOR A MATTRESS, WOVEN INTO MATS AND MADE INTO DOLLS.

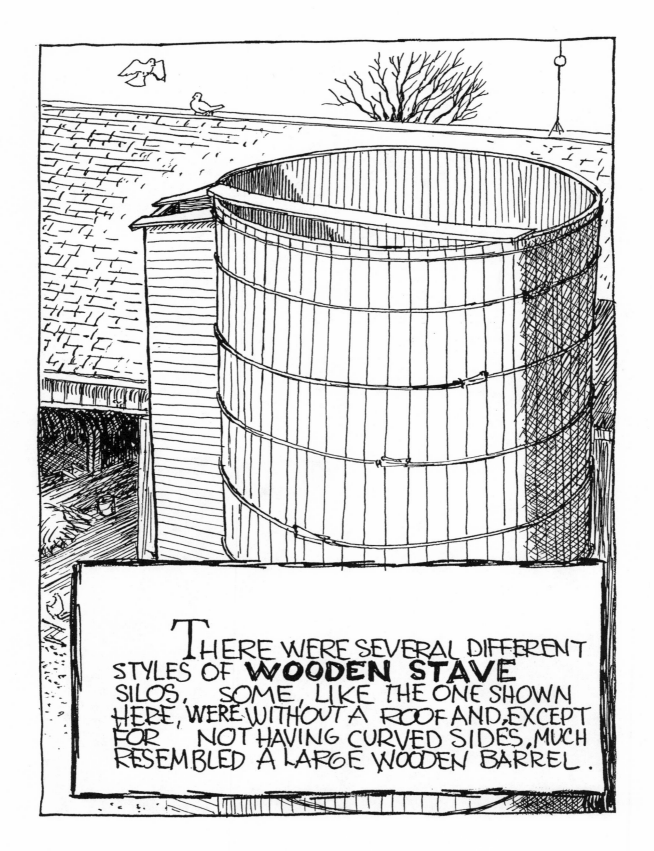

THERE WERE SEVERAL DIFFERENT STYLES OF **WOODEN STAVE** SILOS, SOME, LIKE THE ONE SHOWN HERE, WERE WITHOUT A ROOF AND, EXCEPT FOR NOT HAVING CURVED SIDES, MUCH RESEMBLED A LARGE WOODEN BARREL.

ONE OF THE EARLY SILOS OF THE MIDWEST WAS THAT BUILT OF HOLLOW CLAY TILE. IT HAD A CONCRETE ROOF AND A CHUTE BUILT OF WOOD.

ONE OF THE MOST HANDSOME AND DISTINCTIVE STRUCTURES ON THE RURAL LANDSCAPE, IN THE EARLY PART OF THIS CENTURY, MAY HAVE BEEN THE REINFORCED **CONCRETE** **SILO** THAT IS DEPICTED HERE.

SHOWN HERE IS A SECTION OF **BLOWER PIPE** USED WHEN THE SILO FILLING RIG, MOVED FROM FARM TO FARM, INCLUDED THE PIPE THROUGH WHICH THE CHOPPED SILAGE WAS BLOWN INTO THE SILO, AND WHICH HAD TO BE TAKEN APART AND RE-ASSEMBLED FOR EACH MOVE.

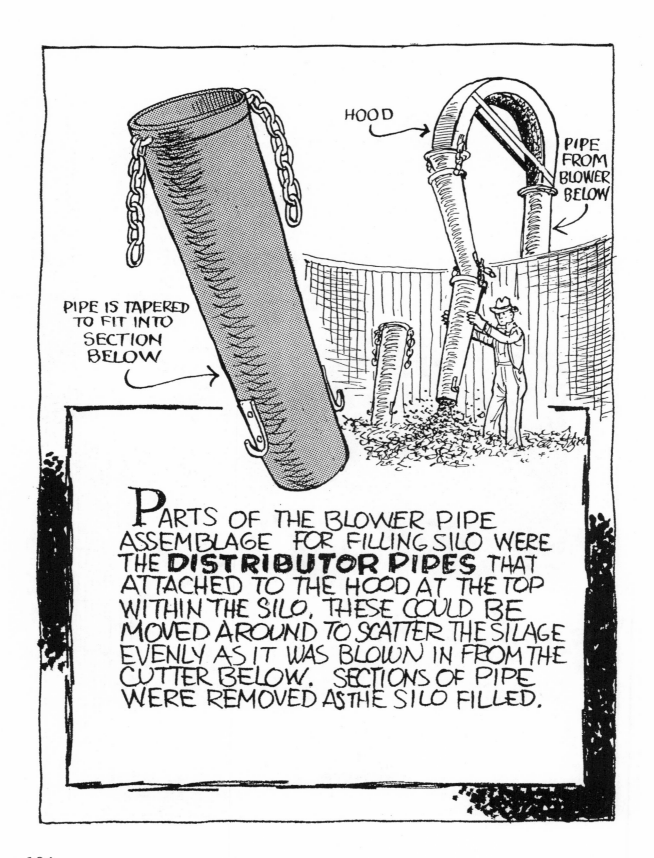

HOOD

PIPE FROM BLOWER BELOW

PIPE IS TAPERED TO FIT INTO SECTION BELOW

Parts of the blower pipe assemblage for filling silo were **the DISTRIBUTOR PIPES** that attached to the hood at the top within the silo, these could be moved around to scatter the silage evenly as it was blown in from the cutter below. Sections of pipe were removed as the silo filled.

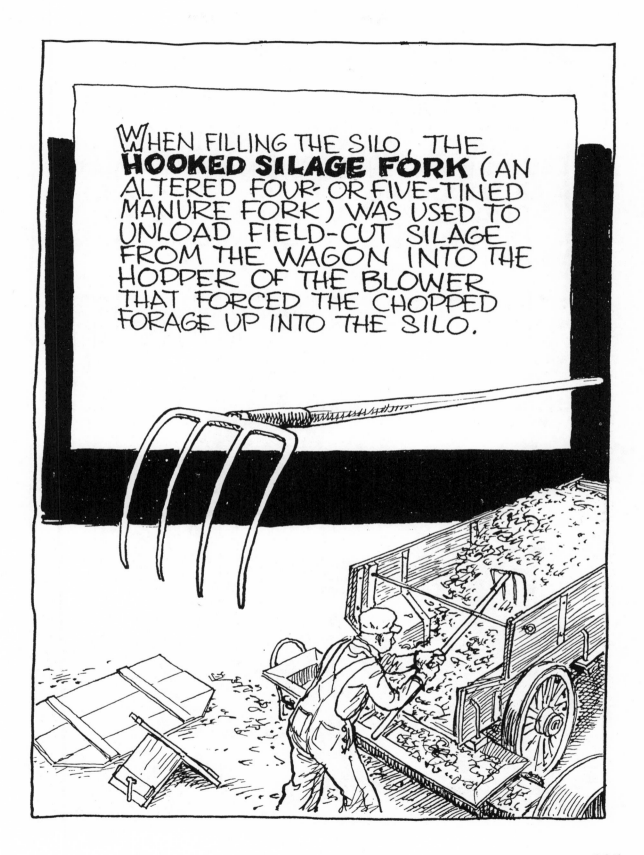

WHEN FILLING THE SILO, THE **HOOKED SILAGE FORK** (AN ALTERED FOUR- OR FIVE-TINED MANURE FORK) WAS USED TO UNLOAD FIELD-CUT SILAGE FROM THE WAGON INTO THE HOPPER OF THE BLOWER THAT FORCED THE CHOPPED FORAGE UP INTO THE SILO.

A JOB THAT OFTEN FELL TO ONE WHO WAS EITHER TOO YOUNG OR TOO OLD TO HANDLE THE HEAVY WORK OF SILO FILLING, WAS THAT OF **"MUDDING IN"** THE SILO DOORS WITH CLAY, SEALING OUT THE AIR TO MINIMIZE SPOILAGE.

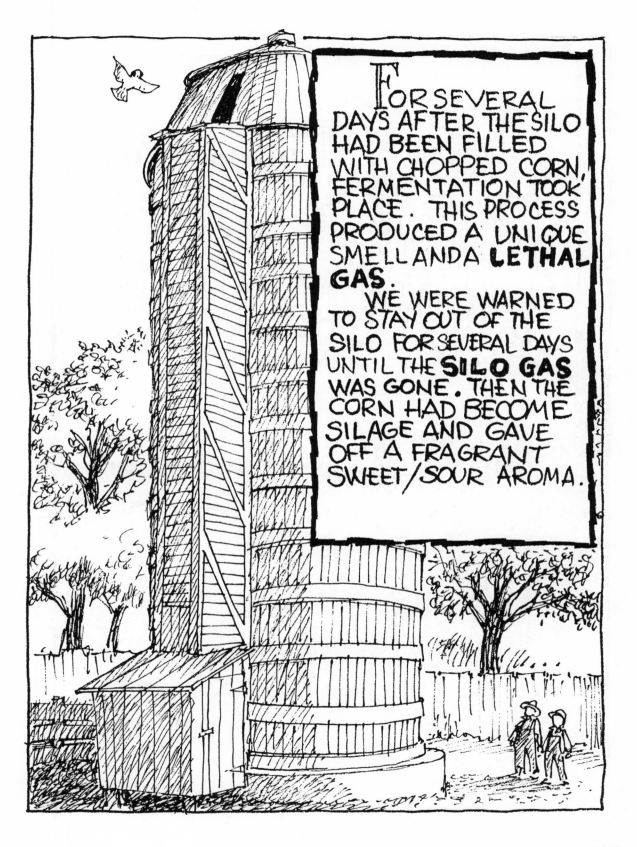

FOR SEVERAL DAYS AFTER THE SILO HAD BEEN FILLED WITH CHOPPED CORN, FERMENTATION TOOK PLACE. THIS PROCESS PRODUCED A UNIQUE SMELL AND A **LETHAL GAS**.

WE WERE WARNED TO STAY OUT OF THE SILO FOR SEVERAL DAYS UNTIL THE **SILO GAS** WAS GONE. THEN THE CORN HAD BECOME SILAGE AND GAVE OFF A FRAGRANT SWEET/SOUR AROMA.

A TOTALLY DIFFERENT KIND OF STRUCTURE IS THE **BUNKER SILO**. THIS VARIATION OF THE PIT SILO PRODUCES THE SAME KIND OF ENSILAGE AS THE VERTICAL CYLINDERS DO. HOWEVER THERE IS MORE SURFACE EXPOSURE TO DRYING AND SPOILAGE THAT MUST BE DEALT WITH. SOME BUNKERS ARE BUILT OF WOOD AS SHOWN HERE, AND SOME OF POURED CONCRETE.

OLD TIRES USED AS BALLAST

Something we don't see anymore, unless it's hanging in the back of some old shed, is the hairpin style **LEAF RAKE** that used to be quite a common item around lawns in the autumn.

110

Almost every farm used to raise chickens. In order to catch the flighty creatures a **CHICKEN HOOK** was devised to catch them by the leg. Usually they were a home-made tool similar to the one shown here.

IN MANY COUNTRY HOMES, IN CLOSETS, BACK ROOMS OR TOOL SHEDS, ONE MIGHT FIND AN OLD **HUNTING JACKET**, SIMILAR TO THE ONE SHOWN HERE. IT MOST LIKELY WOULD BE MADE OF WATER PROOFED KHAKI-COLORED ARMY DUCK MATERIAL CONSISTING OF SHELL LOOPS AND LARGE POCKETS FOR GAME.

IT PROBABLY WOULD HAVE SOME BLOOD STAINS ON IT.

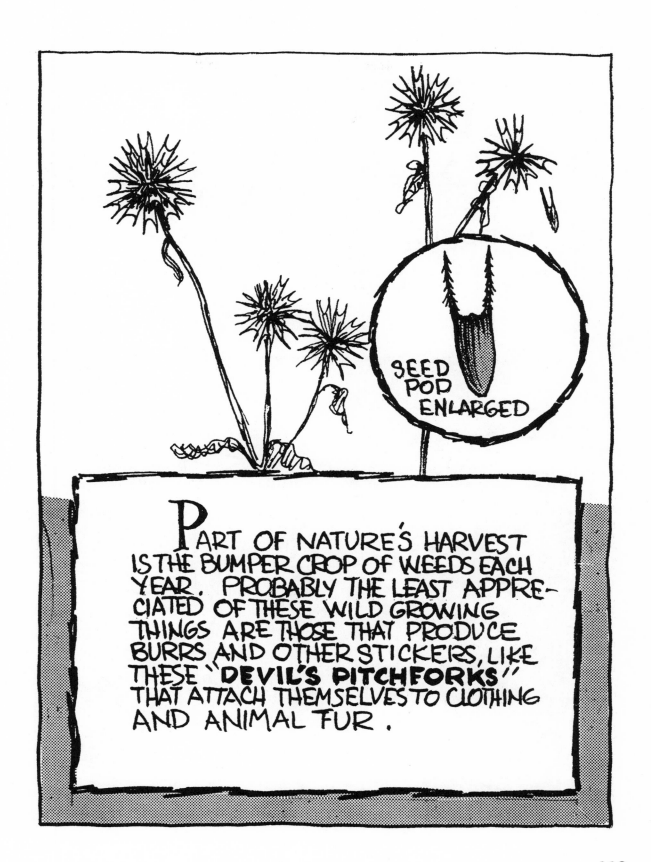

SEED
POD
ENLARGED

PART OF NATURE'S HARVEST IS THE BUMPER CROP OF WEEDS EACH YEAR. PROBABLY THE LEAST APPRECIATED OF THESE WILD GROWING THINGS ARE THOSE THAT PRODUCE BURRS AND OTHER STICKERS, LIKE THESE "**DEVIL'S PITCHFORKS**" THAT ATTACH THEMSELVES TO CLOTHING AND ANIMAL FUR.

A LOOP OF NUMBER NINE GAUGE, GALVANIZED WIRE OFTEN SERVES AS AN IMPROVISED **GATE LATCH** ON FARMYARD, FIELD AND PASTURE GATES.

FOR COOKING IN AN IRON KETTLE OVER AN OPEN FIRE, A **TRIPOD** MADE OF WOODEN POLES, CUT FROM NEAR AT HAND, IS QUITE SATISFACTORY—AS LONG AS THEY ARE POSITIONED A SAFE DISTANCE FROM THE FIRE.

It is hard to surpass, or even to match, the special ambiance created by an **AUTUMN CAMPFIRE** under a **FULL MOON**.

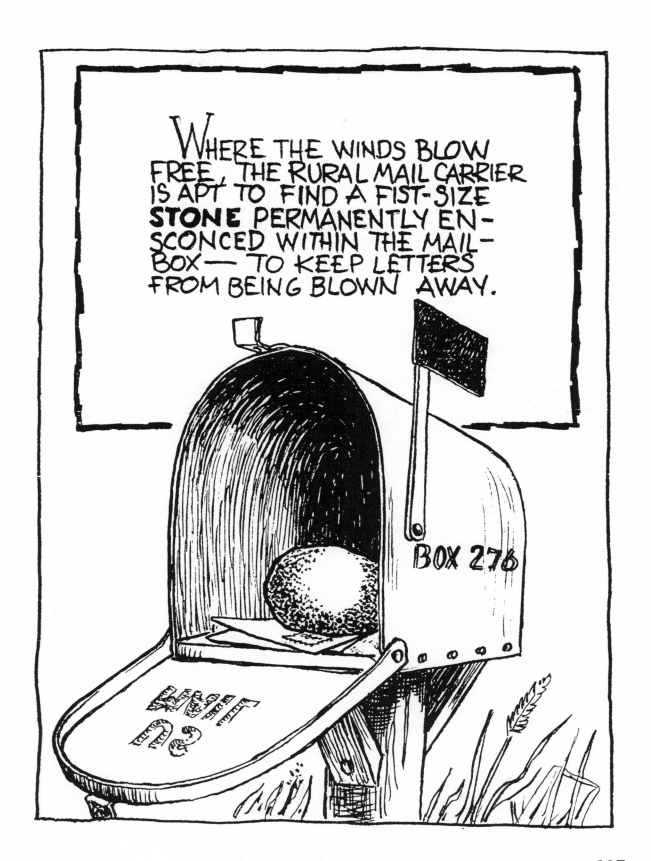

Winter

Contributing to the joy of living where there is a distinct change of seasons is the anticipation with which each season is greeted. Not only did the coming of winter herald the holiday season with its special celebrations, it brought joyful expectation of the first snowfall. Out of a leaden sky would first come a few, intricately designed flakes and then the cold still air would gradually fill with fluffy white crystals floating down with a quiet, whispering sound through the bare tree branches, muffling the fields, groves, and farmsteads in a soft blanket of white.

But winter would also be a time of howling blizzards threatening all creatures on the prairies—humans, farm animals, and wildlife. And it could be a time of breathtaking beauty when a full moon made the snow-covered earth nearly as bright as day.

Winter meant iron-hard cold and hardship, frostbite and chilblains, being confined to bed in sickness with bad-tasting medicine and mustard plasters.

Winter was a time for bundled-up fun outside—snowballs, sledding, skiing, sleigh rides, and ice skating. But it also brought cold-stalled cars and digging out snow-blocked walkways and roads.

The cold time of the year was also a cozy time when many of the wild creatures on the farm were burrowed deep in hibernation, and the farm animals were snug in deeply straw-bedded pens and stalls. The family gathered around the stove to read books, play cards or board games, and eat popcorn and apples. It was a time of togetherness for family and friends, enjoying mugs of hot chocolate or hot cider.

Winter was also when we dreamed and planned for spring.

IN A DARK CORNER OF THE ATTIC OF THE OLD FARM-HOUSE, AMONG OTHER RELICS' OF A DISTANT PAST, IS AN OLD, BLACK IRON **PANCAKE GRIDDLE.** THIS MUCH-USED OLD KITCHEN UTENSIL PLAYED AN IMPORTANT PART IN THE LARGE, TASTY, NOURISHING BREAKFASTS THAT WERE SERVED TO THE FAMILY BACK THEN.

A BREAKFAST THAT REALLY GOT A COUNTRY PERSON GOING ON A COLD WINTER MORNING, WAS ONE THAT INCLUDED **PANCAKES** AND **PORK SAUSAGE GRAVY.**

In the text panel within the image:

IN THE EARLY 1900s, THE **BOBSLED** WAS PROBABLY THE MAIN MEANS OF WINTER TRANS-PORTATION IN FARM COUNTRY, FOR PEOPLE AS WELL AS FOR SUPPLIES.

Sometimes, when an old workhorse died it was recycled, so to speak, by using its hide to make a **HORSEHIDE ROBE**. In this way the warm memory of our old friend and workmate was kept alive as we were kept warm traveling through a cold winter landscape.

THIS ROBE WAS FROM QUEEN, TEAMMATE OF JIM

GREEN FELT TRIM

WOOL CLOTH LINING

WHETHER MADE BY HAND OR BY MACHINE THERE IS SOMETHING ABOUT A **WOODEN SPOON**, AS WELL AS A **CERAMIC MUG**, THAT APPEALS TO THE UNIVERSAL LONGING FOR THAT WHICH IS OF THE EARTH.

When butter-making was a home industry, a wooden **BUTTER MOLD** was often used to make decorated butter patties with which to grace the table at meal-time. — It consisted of a hollow cylinder in which butter was pressed and then pushed out by plunger in which a design had been carved.

DECORATED BASE OF PLUNGER

BUTTER PATTY

BEFORE ELECTRIC REFRIGERATION WAS COMMON, THE ANNUAL **ICE HARVEST** WAS A PART OF THE WINTER SCENE ON LAKES AND PONDS. THE ICE WAS CUT AND STORED IN SAWDUST IN ICE HOUSES FOR USE IN REFRIGERATION IN HOMES AND INDUSTRY DURING THE WARM SEASON.

BACK BEFORE FARM HOUSES WERE MODERNIZED (WITH INDOOR BATHROOMS AND TOILETS), THE **CHAMBER POT** WAS AN ESSENTIAL COMFORT ITEM THAT WAS USUALLY KEPT IN THE PRIVACY OF THE BEDROOM OR CLOSET.

PEOPLE, GENERALLY OF THE "YOUNGER" GENERATION, OR THOSE NOT FAMILIAR WITH RURAL LIFE, ERRONEOUSLY REFER TO ANY OLD COAL OR WOOD BURNING SPACE HEATER AS A **POTBELLIED STOVE**. WRONG. A STOVE WITH THAT NAME HAD A **POT BELLY**, SIMILAR TO THE ONE SHOWN HERE.

COAL WAS OFTEN FED FROM THE TOP

NOW, ISN'T **THIS** A **POT BELLY**?

THESE STOVES, MADE OF HEAVY CAST IRON, WERE OFTEN USED IN RAILROAD DEPOTS AND COUNTRY STORES.

128

ONE OF OUR FAVORITE PIES, DURING THE HOLIDAY SEASON, WAS MOM'S SPECIAL **MINCEMEAT PIE** THAT WAS MADE OF A GROUND-UP MIXTURE OF APPLES, RAISINS, MEAT AND SPICES IN JUST THE RIGHT PROPORTIONS TO MAKE FOR DELICIOUS EATING.

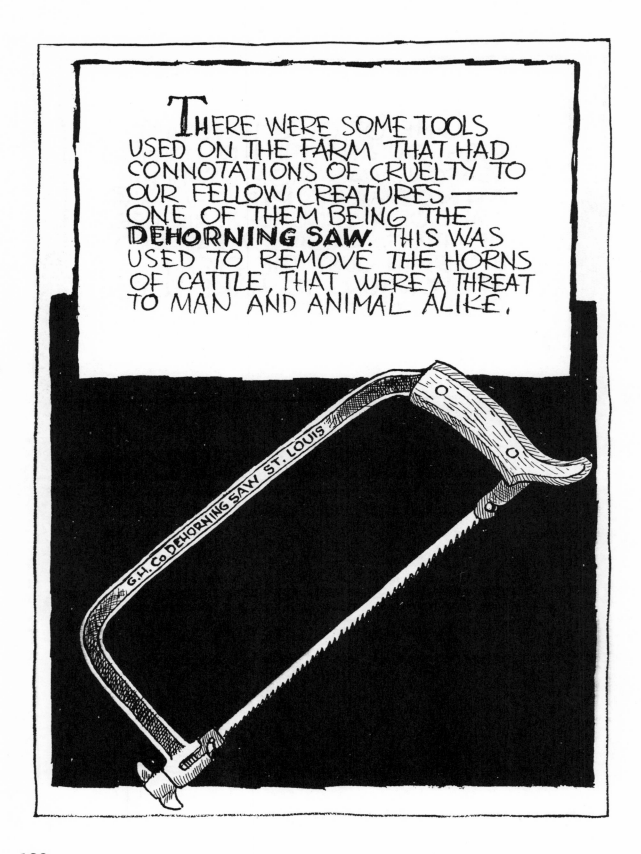

There were some tools used on the farm that had connotations of cruelty to our fellow creatures — one of them being the **DEHORNING SAW.** This was used to remove the horns of cattle, that were a threat to man and animal alike.

WINTER, IN THE COUNTRY, IS A TIME FOR SPECIAL JOBS, LIKE SPLITTING FIREWOOD OR OLD-TIME FENCE RAILS, AS IS DEPICTED HERE. (WOOD SPLITS EASIER DURING BELOW-FREEZING TEMPERATURES.)

A FEED BUNK, MADE OF HEAVY PLANKS AND TIMBERS, HELD TOGETHER WITH BOLTS AND STEEL RODS, WAS USED FOR FEEDING CATTLE SILAGE OR MIXED GROUND GRAIN.

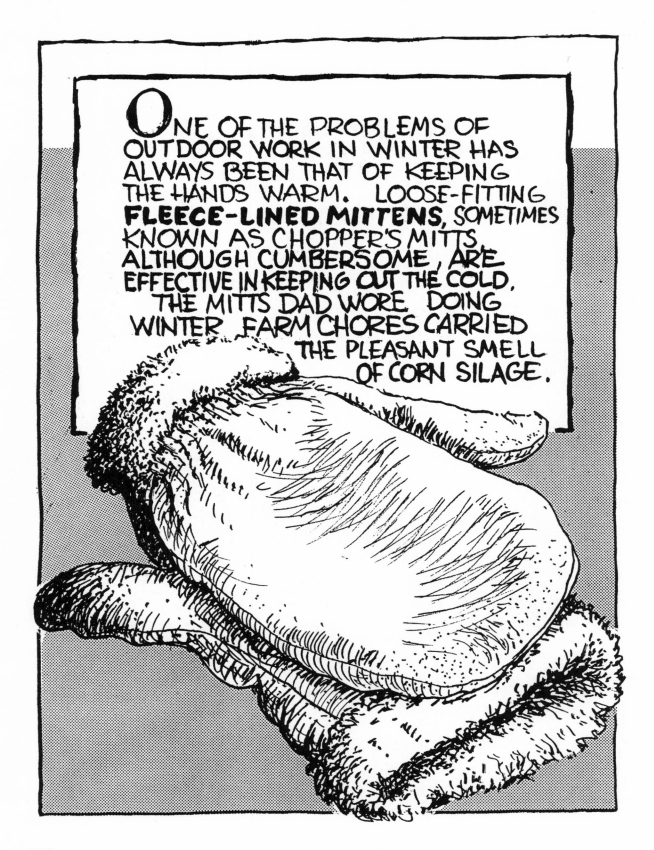

One of the problems of outdoor work in winter has always been that of keeping the hands warm. Loose-fitting **FLEECE-LINED MITTENS**, sometimes known as chopper's mitts although cumbersome, are effective in keeping out the cold. The mitts Dad wore doing winter farm chores carried the pleasant smell of corn silage.

ALONG ABOUT MARCH, WHILE THE WEATHER WAS STILL WINTERLIKE, THE **BUTCHERING TOOLS** WERE ASSEMBLED FOR THE ANNUAL HOG BUTCHERING TO PROVIDE FOR THE SEASON'S SUPPLY OF FRESH PORK, CURED BACON AND HAMS AND JARS OF SAUSAGE AND LARD.

138

WHEN HORSE-DRAWN SLEDS WERE THE MAIN MEANS OF WINTER TRAVEL, IT WAS IMPORTANT TO KEEP THE ROAD SNOW-PACKED FOR GOOD SLEDDING. A HORSE-DRAWN **SNOW PACKER** WAS ONE IMPLEMENT USED FOR THIS PURPOSE.

FILLED WITH SAND

When snowfall is heavy, it sometimes becomes quite necessary to remove the excess weight from some roofs. A simple homemade, long handled **SNOW RAKE** proves a useful tool for this task

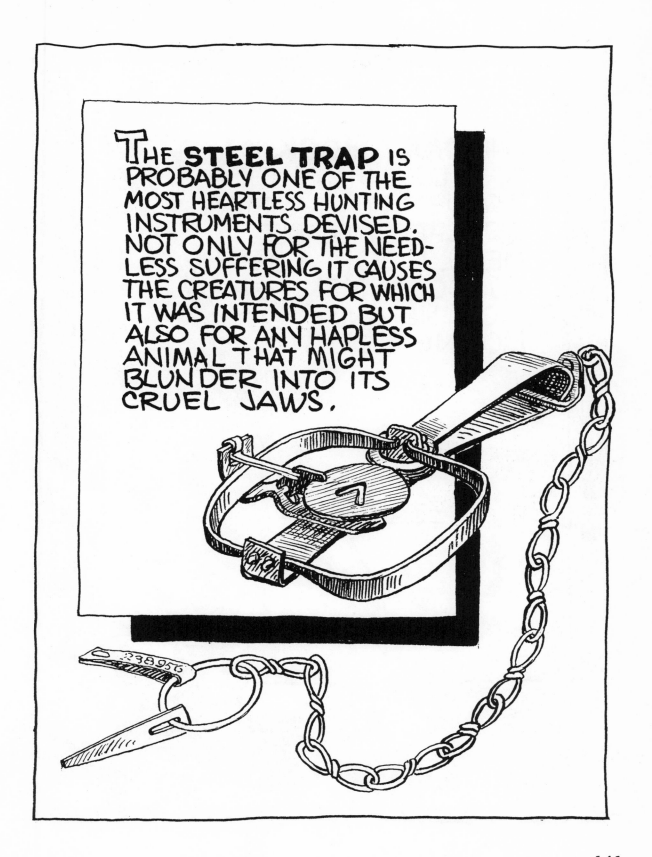

The **STEEL TRAP** is probably one of the most heartless hunting instruments devised. Not only for the needless suffering it causes the creatures for which it was intended but also for any hapless animal that might blunder into its cruel jaws.

A FAMILIAR OBJECT IN OUR FARM KITCHEN WAS THE BATTERED **COAL HOD**, WHICH WAS USED IN FEEDING THE VORACIOUS APPETITE OF THE BIG, BLACK RANGE THAT BURNED COAL, WOOD OR CORN COBS.